AN ANTHOLOGY OF

AND MINERALS

AN ANTHOLOGY OF

Rocks

AND MINERALS

Written by Dr. Devin Dennie
Illustrated by Angela Rizza and Olivier Ribbe

Contents

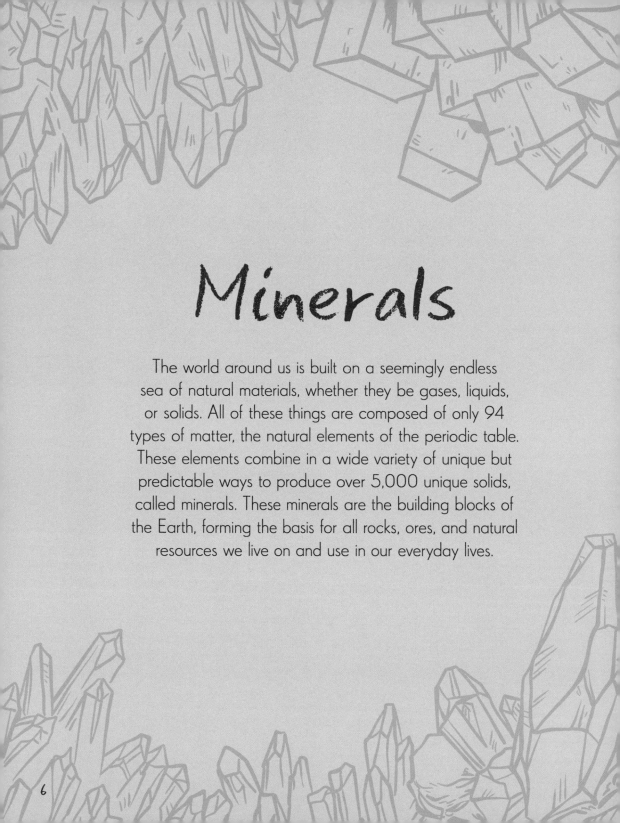

Minerals

The world around us is built on a seemingly endless sea of natural materials, whether they be gases, liquids, or solids. All of these things are composed of only 94 types of matter, the natural elements of the periodic table. These elements combine in a wide variety of unique but predictable ways to produce over 5,000 unique solids, called minerals. These minerals are the building blocks of the Earth, forming the basis for all rocks, ores, and natural resources we live on and use in our everyday lives.

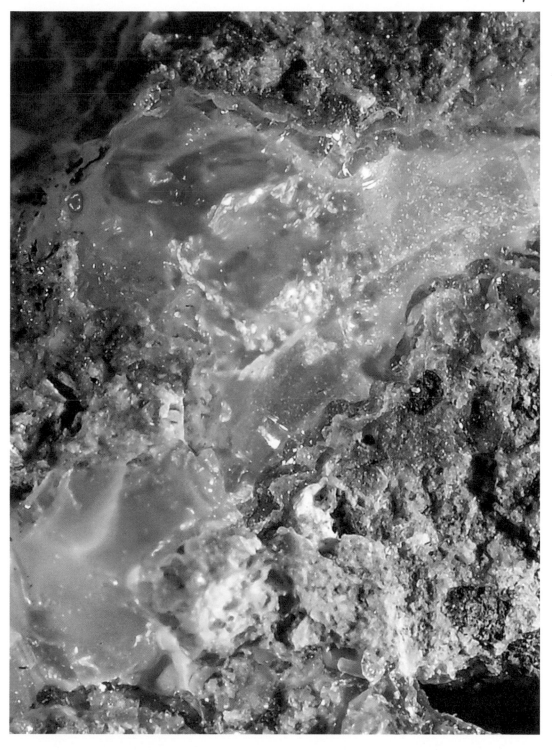

What is a mineral?

If the Earth were a brick building, rocks would be the bricks that form it, and minerals would be the materials that create the bricks. Minerals are inorganic, which means they do not come from plants or animals. They are made up of chemicals that combine in almost infinite ways to form the world we see around us. Minerals help build the many resources we use and depend on every day.

A mineral is a solid substance that forms in nature, such as this cassiterite.

Minerals have a defined recipe, or makeup. Each type of mineral is made of the same kind and amount of chemicals.

Most minerals have a recurring crystallized shape with an internal orderly arrangement.

Many minerals keep the same crystal shape even when they break.

Mohs' hardness scale

In 1812, German scientist Friedrich Mohs created a scale to measure the hardness of minerals relative to one another. The Mohs' hardness scale is still used today to help us name and classify minerals. The hardest value on the scale is 10, represented by a diamond, and the softest mineral is 1, which is talc. All other minerals lie somewhere in between.

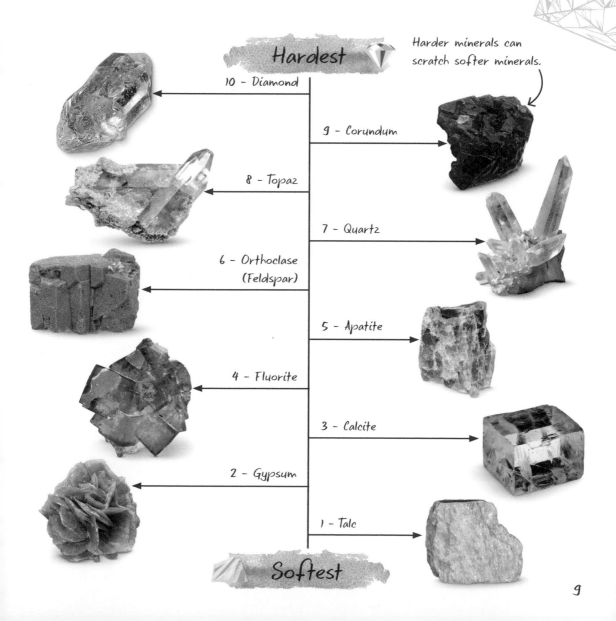

Hardest

Harder minerals can scratch softer minerals.

10 – Diamond

9 – Corundum

8 – Topaz

7 – Quartz

6 – Orthoclase (Feldspar)

5 – Apatite

4 – Fluorite

3 – Calcite

2 – Gypsum

1 – Talc

Softest

Types of minerals

Minerals are grouped into families based on their composition. Minerals in a particular group often share a common makeup, and contain similar chemical elements. So, for example, all minerals in the silicate group contain the element silica. There are eight main groups of minerals.

Native elements

Most minerals are made from combinations of chemical elements, but a few, such as silver and gold, occur naturally by themselves. These are called native elements.

Native gold

Quartz (left) and feldspar (right) are the most common silicates.

Carbonate mineral, dolomite

Silicates

The most common group of minerals are the silicates, which all contain silica.

Carbonates

Carbonates are based on carbon and oxygen—crucial for life on Earth!

Cinnabar is a sulfide made with mercury.

Sulfate mineral, gypsum

Sulfides

Sulfur combines with different metals to form sulfides.

Sulfates

Minerals containing both sulfur and oxygen are called sulfates.

Spinel is a ruby-red oxide crystal.

Phosphate mineral, apatite

Oxides

Oxides are minerals that contain metals, such as iron, and oxygen.

Phosphates

Minerals made from phosphorus and oxygen are called phosphates.

Rock salt (halite) is a common halide.

Halides

Minerals that contain halogen elements make up the group called halides.

Talc

Mohs' scale: 1

Measuring just 1 on the Mohs' scale, talc is the softest mineral in the world. A type of clay, talc can scratch easily, and is smooth and powdery to the touch. This makes this metamorphic mineral very adaptable. Talc is used in a lot of things, from makeup and toiletries to paint and ceramics.

A lump of talc is known as soapstone.

Colors range from whitish gray to green.

Molybdenite

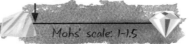

Mohs' scale: 1–1.5

S lippery and shiny, molybdenite is a mineral made from the metal molybdenum mixed with sulfur. It is used in electronics, and its crystals can conduct electricity even when they are only a few atoms thick.

Molybdenite is extremely soft, and looks and feels a lot like graphite. You can even use it to draw with!

Metallic luster, with a unique hexagon-shaped crystal

Dark, lead-like color

Graphite

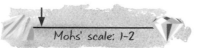
This mineral is composed entirely of the element carbon. Carbon is the same element that makes up all living things, including, plants, animals, and of course—people!

Graphite is a very soft, black mineral, and is used to make a lot of products, including pencils. Interestingly, graphite is not actually a metal, but unlike all other non-metals, it can conduct electricity.

Very soft, and scratchable with a fingernail

Notes

· Forms from the changing nature, or metamorphism, of shale or coal, and from limestone

· Superb lubricant because it is made up of many tiny layers that glide easily across one another

Metallic luster

Dark-gray to black color

Realgar

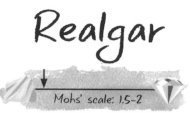

Mohs' scale: 1.5–2

Danger! Do not ever swallow or inhale realgar, as it is toxic. This mineral is composed of arsenic and sulfur, and was used for thousands of years as a pigment, a medicine, and even as an assassin's poison!

Realgar is also called "ruby sulfur" because of its vivid red crystals, and was once a common ingredient in the poison used to kill rats and mice.

Over time, when left exposed to light, realgar breaks down into a yellow powder called pararealgar.

Resin-like to brilliant luster

Very soft mineral

Red-orange color

Muscovite

Mohs' scale: 2–2.5

Crystals can be split to form extremely thin, flexible sheets that can be peeled down.

This mineral can form in layers of light colored flat and bendable sheets, like the pages in a book. Long ago, muscovite was used both in Russia and North America to make window panes. In Russia, it was mined near Moscow, and the glass was called "Muscovy glass"—hence the name "muscovite." The mineral has a subtle pearly luster and can add sparkle to paints, ceramic glazes, and makeup.

Notes

· Important insulator against fire and is used in electronics and power cables

· Glitter in paint is often made from tiny flakes of muscovite mica!

Reflective with a glassy luster and a mild sheen, like a pearl

Translucent to transparent, and colorless to lightly tinted

Sulfur is very soft and its crystals have flat surfaces.

Pure sulfur is a bright, almost neon, yellow color.

Sulfur

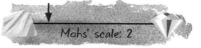

Mohs' scale: 2

Pure, native sulfur is a vivid yellow mineral that can give off an unpleasant smell like rotten eggs! It most often forms in active volcanic areas—especially near hot springs, geysers, or in openings in the Earth called fumaroles, which spout hot, sulfurous gases. Sulfur has many uses, including the making of sulfuric acid, which is incredibly important in industry worldwide.

Gypsum crystals sometimes form flower-like shapes called desert roses.

Grains of sand get mixed into the gypsum.

Several desert roses can clump together to form a bouquet.

Gypsum

Mohs' scale: 2

I f salty seawater dries out and evaporates in a hot place, it can leave behind a mineral called gypsum. This soft mineral is very common and is extremely useful. A symbol of purity and beauty, the ancient Mesopotamians used it to create alabaster carvings. Today, gypsum is added to water to make plaster for building work.

Stibnite

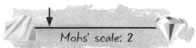

Mohs' scale: 2

Stibnite is a type of sulfide mineral that contains the part-metal substance known as antimony, which is toxic. It is a soft mineral with a metallic luster, like polished steel.

Stibnite can be found as long, thin crystals that can actually be bent and twisted in your hands without breaking.

Notes

· Relatively rare mineral, yet major source of the element antimony

· Antimony was used in ancient times as a cosmetic— the ancient Egyptians often wore it as an eyeliner

· Important element for alchemists, and was used in experiments by the ancient Greeks and Romans

Often forms radiating clusters of long, thin crystals

Lead-like gray color with a bright metallic luster

Borax

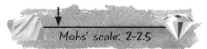

Mohs' scale: 2–2.5

The word "borax" comes from an Arabic word *buraq*, meaning "white." And, true to its name, borax is a snowy white powder, which dissolves in water.

Borax was first discovered many centuries ago in dry lakebeds in Tibet. Today, the mineral is found in many areas, including the USA, Turkey, and Chile.

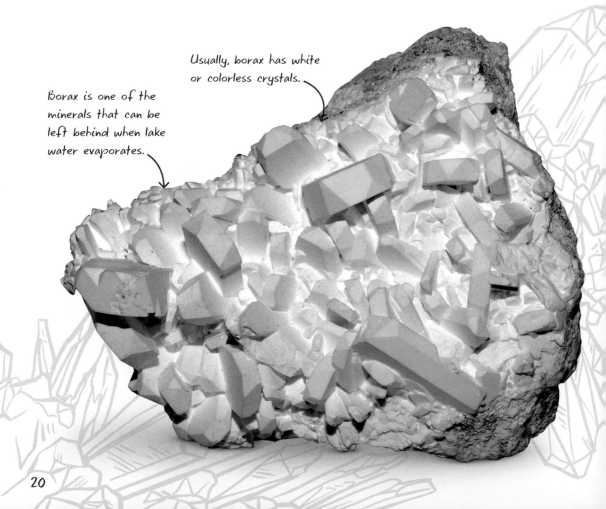

Usually, borax has white or colorless crystals.

Borax is one of the minerals that can be left behind when lake water evaporates.

Halite

Mohs' scale: 2–2.5

Commonly known as rock salt or table salt, halite is a mineral we eat almost every day. It is usually found in sedimentary rocks and is formed after seawater has evaporated, or turned to vapor. Because of its widespread use as a seasoning and preservative, halite is one of the most important minerals in the world.

Grows into perfect cube-shaped crystals

Halite is quite soft, and so is easily scratched.

Notes

· Made mostly of sodium and chlorine

· Often found alongside other minerals that form from water evaporating, such as anhydrite, sylvite, and gypsum

· It is used to remove snow and ice from roads and pavements in freezing-cold weather

Cinnabar is heated in furnaces to release elemental mercury, also known as quicksilver.

Cinnabar's dark-red crystals were once used to make a pigment called vermilion.

The mineral is made up of equal amounts of the elements mercury and sulfur.

Cinnabar

Mohs' scale: 2-2.5

This stunning mineral is well-named. The word "cinnabar" comes from Persian and Arabic words meaning "dragon's blood," reflecting its deep-red color. Cinnabar is a common ore of mercury, a metal that is liquid at room temperature.

Cinnabar's brilliant-red color meant that it was once used in painting, though it was later found to be highly poisonous. The mineral often forms around volcanic vents and hot springs.

Rainbow-like play of colors on the surface

Mostly dark gray in color, also very dense

Bismuth

Mohs' scale: 2-2.5

Bismuth is a rare metal with unique characteristics. It occurs both as a native element, and also forms crystals like a mineral. It has a very low melting temperature. When bismuth is exposed to air, the light reflects beautiful rainbows of color on its surface!

Notes

· One of the few elements that expand rather than shrink when freezing

· Bismuth looks like lead, but, unlike this metal, is non-toxic

· Unlike many metals, such as iron, bismuth is repelled by magnets rather than attracted to them

Artinite

Mohs' scale: 2.5

Rich in magnesium, this mineral also contains water, carbon, and oxygen. Artinite is unique in that it often forms soft, rounded balls of crystal needles. This brittle and delicate mineral is found in hydrothermal waters, which means the water has been heated within the rocks found below the surface of the Earth.

Delicate, needle-like crystals

Soft, rounded clusters look like cotton wool.

Dark-gray color with a distinct metallic luster

Perfect cubic-shaped crystal faces

One of the most dense (heaviest) minerals on Earth

Galena

Mohs' scale: 2.5–2.75

O ne of the earliest minerals ever used in human civilization, galena was popular with the ancient Egyptians and Romans as a source of lead for making pipes, coins, and other items.

With its striking six- to eight-sided crystals, galena is a common sulfide mineral. It is the main ore that contains lead, and is an important source for silver, too. Galena is found all over the world.

Gold

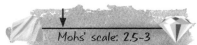

Mohs' scale: 2.5–3

When you imagine gold nuggets, you are thinking of pure, native gold. This soft, yellow metal has been highly prized since early times. Gold is often found in its native state, untouched by other elements—this is because of its ability to remain intact, and not react with other chemicals. Gold almost never tarnishes, so it is highly valued both as jewelry, and as a form of currency.

Notes

· Excellent conductor of electricity, so is often used in electronic devices such as computers, TVs, and mobile phones

· Like copper, it can be stretched into thin layers or wires

· Important metal used in today's spacecraft and satellites, as it is reliable and long-lasting

Gets rounded into nuggets in streams and rivers

Gold is soft, and it can be easily shaped with tools.

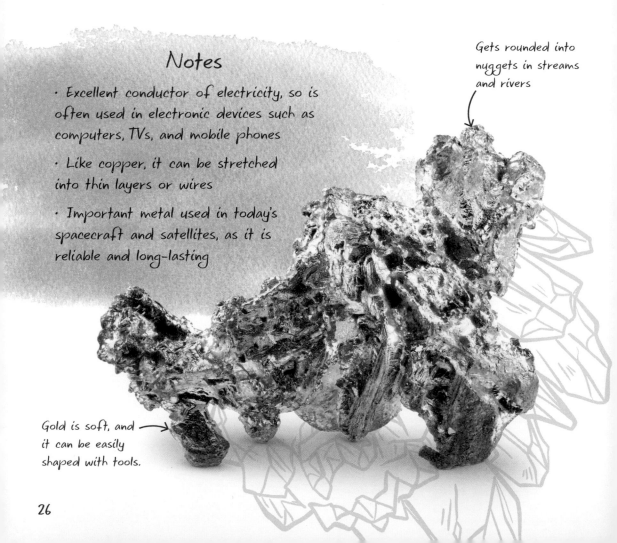

Lepidolite

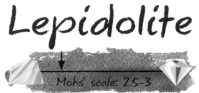

Mohs' scale: 2.5–3

The valuable and rare mineral lepidolite contains a mixture of elements, the most important one being lithium, which is also a metal. Lithium is an important material in much of today's high-tech electronics, including rechargeable batteries. Lepidolite is also used to make glass, enamels, and ornamental stone.

Often made of rock-like clusters of small, plate-like crystals

Lepidolite is often purple, or it can be pink to gray.

Vanadinite

Mohs' scale: 2.5-3

The rare and delicate mineral vanadinite forms six-sided, or hexagonal-shaped, crystals. Vanadinite was first discovered in Mexico, and has since been found in arid places around the world, including Morocco, and Arizona and New Mexico in the USA.

Vanadinite is the source of the metal vanadium, which strengthens steel and toughens tools, such as wrenches and knives. The mineral's lovely warm shades are used to color glass and ceramics.

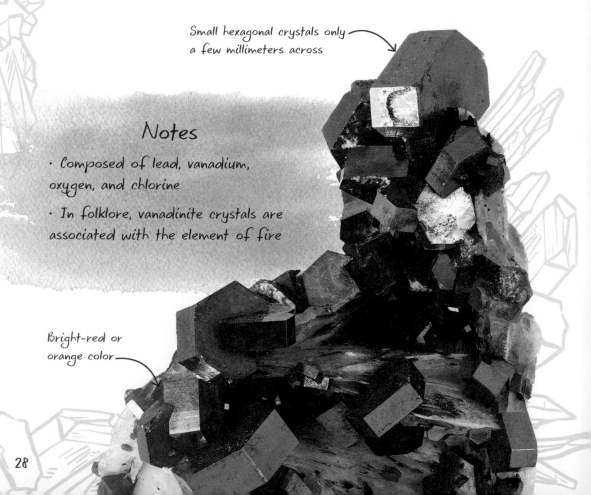

Small hexagonal crystals only a few millimeters across

Notes

· Composed of lead, vanadium, oxygen, and chlorine

· In folklore, vanadinite crystals are associated with the element of fire

Bright-red or orange color

If you look through calcite, it bends light (refracts), making a kind of double vision!

Iceland spar is a popular variety of calcite that is transparent.

Calcite

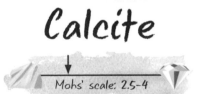

Mohs' scale: 2.5-4

The soft, carbonate mineral calcite is very common, and is second only to quartz at the surface of the Earth. It is found in limestone—especially in the ocean floor, lake beds, riverbeds, by hot springs, and in caves. Amazingly, if you add hydrochloric acid to calcite, it will fizz, like soda!

Pearl

Like, for example, jet, pearls are mineraloids, as they come from living, organic materials. Pearls are found in shelled mollusks, such as oysters. The inside shell of an oyster gets coated with a material called nacre. When a grain of sand enters the shell, it gets covered in the nacre layer by layer, like a lollipop. As the layers accumulate, they make a round nodule—this is the pearl!

Pearls vary depending on the kind of mollusk and the type of water the mollusk lives in.

As well as white, pearls come in a wide range of colors, including pink, black, and gold.

Pearls can be round, oval, or even oblong, depending on how they formed.

Wulfenite

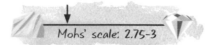

Mohs' scale: 2.75-3

The mineral wulfenite usually forms from lead, and it also often contains elements such as molybdenum. The mix of lead and molybdenum gives the mineral its unique, bright colors, which can be bright-orange, yellow, or red, too. Because of its striking appearance, wulfenite is a popular collector's mineral and is often used as a gemstone.

Notes

· Can be used as a shield against radiation

· Some of the finest specimens come from the Red Cloud Mine in Yuma, Arizona, which has produced some of the largest, well-formed crystals

Crystals are thin and flat, and can be square-, rectangular-, or pyramid-shaped.

Bright yellow-orange to orange-red colored crystals

Serpentine

Mohs' scale: 3-4

Serpentine is the name of a group of minerals that are mostly composed of magnesium, iron, and silicon. Serpentine minerals are often used as gemstones and in carving, due to their attractive green to blue-green colors and waxy luster.

Another name for serpentine is "new jade" or "Suzhou jade," because it was historically used as a substitute for jade in Chinese art.

Lizardite

Chrysotile

Antigorite is an important mineral belonging to the serpentine group.

There are many varieties of serpentine, including lizardite and chrysotile.

Glassy, and dark green in color

Bornite

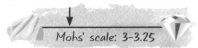

Mohs' scale: 3–3.25

Also known as "peacock ore," bornite has sparkling purple, blue, and gold colors that look a little like the feathers of a peacock. This copper-iron sulfide mineral has a metallic luster and a red-brown to brass color. It is a major ore of copper, and a minor ore of nickel and cobalt.

Notes

- Often found alongside other sulfide minerals, such as chalcopyrite, pyrite, or marcasite

- Forms in all three types of rock; igneous, metamorphic, and sedimentary

A shimmering mix of blue, purple, and gold occurs where bornite is weathered.

Pale-colored crystals

Sometimes forms in delicate, snowflake shapes

Cerussite

Mohs' scale: 3-3.5

Sometimes also called "white lead," cerussite forms colorless-to-white crystals. The mineral is commonly found alongside copper and silver deposits in Australia, Europe, and the USA. Once the key ingredient in lead paint, cerussite is poisonous and so is no longer used.

Baryte

Mohs' scale: 3-3.5

The stunning mineral baryte can form beautiful petal shapes. It is one of the densest non-metal minerals on Earth, and occurs in a variety of conditions, including sedimentary rocks that are rich in clay and limestone. Baryte has been used for many years as a white pigment, and as a filler in paper and cloth-making.

Notes

· Baryte is important in radiology, a branch of medicine that uses imaging technology to detect and treat diseases

· Used in oil and gas production and in the making of paints, plastics, and rubber

· Also known as "heavy spar"

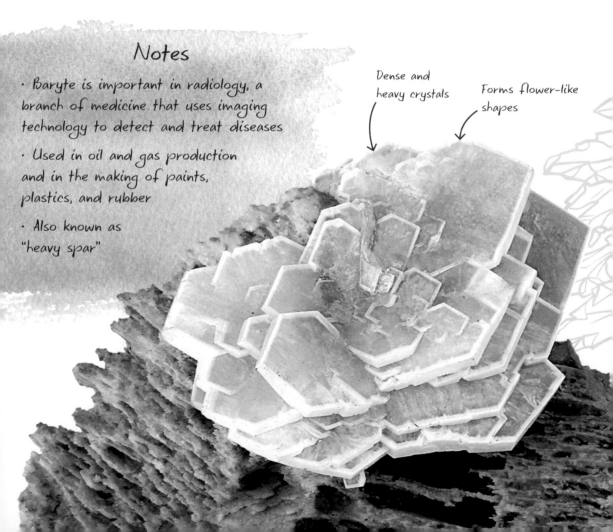

Dense and heavy crystals

Forms flower-like shapes

Jet is often carved into beads, pendants, and other decorative objects.

It is soft, yet strong enough to carve into jewelry.

Solid black, with a dull, earthy luster

Jet

Mohs' scale: 2.5-4

Unlike many gemstones, jet is not a true mineral, but rather a mineral-like substance called a mineraloid. Jet is formed from fossilized wood—this is when ancient tree trunks rot and compress over thousands of years, eventually turning into carbon-rich material. Polished jet gemstones have a unique beauty, and are often used in jewelry-making and art.

Forms tiny crystals

Gray, bronze to brassy colors

Pentlandite

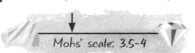

Mohs' scale: 3.5–4

Pentlandite was first discovered in a huge impact crater called Sudbury Basin in Ontario, Canada, in the 19th century, and was named after the Irish geologist who found it—Joseph Barclay Pentland. This metallic mineral contains both iron and nickel, and is typically found in shades of bronze or brass.

Malachite

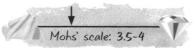

Mohs' scale: 3.5–4

When polished and cut, malachite looks a little like frozen green smoke! It's a beautiful mineral that forms colorful swirled patterns in many shades of green, emerging in streaks and circles throughout the stone. Strangely enough, malachite is full of copper, which is brown in its pure, native form.

Swirling bands of green

The patterns in malachite are formed from copper-rich carbonate rocks that are shaped by water.

Notes

- Commonly found in Central Africa, Russia, Australia, and Mexico
- Revered by many early civilizations, including the ancient Egyptians
- Is said to ward off illness and threats of danger

Azurite can be made into powder for use as a blue pigment.

When exposed to light or heat, azurite will often turn green and convert to malachite.

Azurite is a deep-blue color.

Azurite

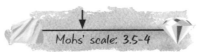

Mohs' scale: 3.5-4

This vivid blue mineral contains copper, carbon, and oxygen. Like its close cousin, malachite, azurite forms from the weathering of copper carbonate deposits. It is found in a wide variety of places, and its shape varies from cloud-like banded bulbs to multicolored crystals.

The crystals are delicate and lacy in appearance, and form in clusters.

Often forms in vugs, or cavities, in volcanic rocks, and in cracks in the Earth containing very hot hydrothermal water.

Stilbite

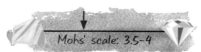

Mohs' scale: 3.5-4

A type of silicate mineral called a zeolite, stilbite forms in white- or peach-colored clusters. Its delicate appearance makes it popular among collectors.

This mineral has a lot of pores, or holes, which means it can trap and release water molecules.

Forms distinctive crystals
with four flat faces

Brassy yellow color
with a metallic luster

Chalcopyrite

Mohs' scale: 3.5–4

Chalcopyrite is a mineral made up
of copper, iron, and sulfur. It is also
known as copper pyrite or yellow copper ore.
It is the most important mineral that contains
copper, and it is the main source for most
of the world's copper production.

Notes

· Forms in igneous rock in heated
hydrothermal water found in
cracks, or veins, underground

· Also found in some sedimentary
rock, and occasionally in
metamorphic rock

· Can give off sulfur dioxide
gas, and can affect breathing if
inhaled as dust

Fluorite

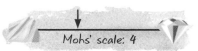

Mohs' scale: 4

*C*olorful fluorite is often found near deposits of valuable metals, such as lead or silver. This makes fluorite a useful indicator mineral, as it signals that treasures may be discovered nearby!

An Irish scientist named George Stokes noticed that fluorite gave off a blue glow under ultraviolet light—and he came up with the word "fluorescence," after the mineral fluorite.

Fluorite has an array of colors, including green, blue, yellow, and purple. It can also be clear.

Some fluorite is made up of bands, or zones, of different colors. This is called zoning.

Rhodochrosite

↓

Mohs' scale: 3.5–4.5

The brilliant reddish-pink mineral called rhodochrosite gets its name from the Greek word *rhodokhros*, which means "of rosy color." The mineral is made up of the elements carbon, manganese, and oxygen, and the gems it produces are extremely valuable.

Rhodochrosite is commonly used as a gemstone, and is prized for its vibrant color and transparency.

Known for its distinctive pink to red color, caused by the presence of manganese

Minerals that glow

Fluorescence

Some rocks and minerals give off light when exposed to ultraviolet (UV) radiation. This phenomenon is called fluorescence. It occurs when a mineral or rock absorbs ultraviolet rays, and then immediately emits lights of different colors, making them look almost unrecognizable!

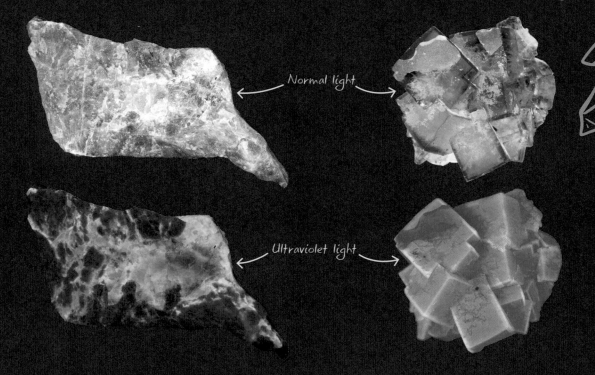

Normal light

Ultraviolet light

Sodalite is usually blue to blue-gray in color, and yet it turns bright orange under UV light! One type of rare fluorescent sodalite, called yooperlite, is found in the Upper Peninsula near Lake Michigan, USA.

Fluorite is often purply pink or green in color. Under fluorescent light, its colors transform from blue to purple to yellow-green depending on the impurities in the crystal.

Phosphorescence

Sometimes, a mineral or rock continues to emit light after the UV radiation source has been removed. This is known as phosphorescence. Like a glow-in-the-dark toy, a phosphorescent mineral releases the absorbed energy slowly over time, resulting in a long-lasting glow.

Normal light

Phosphorescing

Calcite is a common mineral found throughout the world. When it glows, it can give off beautiful blue, red, or orange hues. Calcite can be either fluorescent or phosphorescent.

Under ultraviolet light, the mineral **willemite** can be either phosphorescent or fluorescent. Here, the green glowing parts are the willemite and the orangey parts are calcite.

Wolframite

Mohs' scale: 4–4.5

Popular with collectors, wolframite is a rare mineral with interestingly shaped crystals. It is the most important ore of tungsten— a metal with a high melting point and density. Wolframite is made up of a mixture of elements, including iron and manganese.

Wolframite comes in a variety of colors, including brownish-black, reddish-brown, and grayish-black.

Shiny, metallic luster

Notes

· Typically found in layers of igneous quartz and often associated with ores of molybdenum and tin

· Has a wide range of industrial uses, including cutting tools, electrical goods, and ammunition

· China is a major producer of tungsten; other top producers include Russia, Vietnam, Canada, Bolivia, and Rwanda

Smithsonite

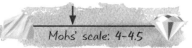

Mohs' scale: 4–4.5

This brittle mineral is quite fragile and can chip easily. It is an ore of zinc, and may be found alongside its lookalike cousin—the mineral hemimorphite. Smithsonite is named after James Smithson, a British chemist and mineralogist who first identified it and who founded the Smithsonian Institution in Washington, DC.

Crystals have a glassy to pearly luster.

Occurs in a spectrum of shades such as green and blue, and also white, yellow, pink, purple, or gray

Red-brown, brown-yellow to green-yellow colored

Greasy to glassy luster

Hexagonal-shaped crystals

Bastnaesite

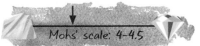

Mohs' scale: 4-4.5

Bastnaesite is a rare but valuable mineral that contains a mixture of three elements—cesium, lanthanum, and yttrium—which are part of a group of unusual metals known as the rare earths. This group is set to play a key role in future technology, and bastnaesite—along with monazite—may become two of the most important minerals in society.

Apatite

Mohs' scale: 5

Apatites are a group of minerals that come in a variety of shapes and colors. An apatite is a rare example of a true mineral that can form from natural biological processes, such as in rich organic material in a shale rock. Apatite is the main source of phosphorus, which is an important nutrient for plants and animals.

Notes

· Often used in the production of fertilizers, and some types of glass and ceramics

· Apatite is found in many different parts of the world, including North America, Brazil, and Russia

· Apatite crystals as heavy as 441 lb (200 kg) have been found in Canada!

Crystals are typically green, blue, or yellow in color.

Glassy or waxy luster

Fluorapophyllite

Mohs' scale: 4.5–5

The apophyllite mineral called fluorapophyllite is often found in volcanic rocks that are formed from potassium-rich magma, such as basalt. As the mineral cools and crystallizes from the hot, liquid magma, it fills holes and fractures in the rock. Fluorapophyllite is a relatively rare mineral, and is mostly found in India, Canada, and the USA.

The crystals form pyramid-like shapes, with a pearly to glassy luster.

Often colored green, yellow, or white, sometimes pink, and even colorless

Notes

· Sometimes used as a gemstone, and can be cut into faceted (many sided) stones or rounded jewels, called cabochons

· Apophyllite is a mineral cousin of zeolite, which contains microscopic holes and can act like a molecular filter, or sieve, that can microscopically filter air or water

Fluorapatite

Mohs' scale: 5

A type of apatite, green fluorapatite is a very useful mineral. It is found in teeth that have been exposed to the fluoride in toothpaste, and it is used in dental repairs. Because it contains the element fluorine, fluorapatite glows under ultraviolet (UV) light!

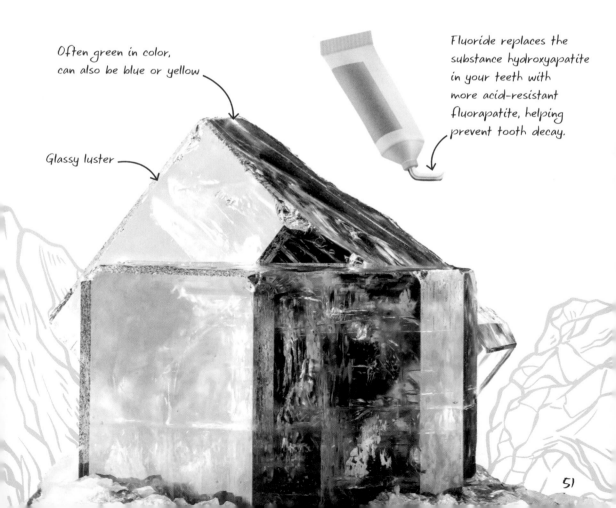

Often green in color, can also be blue or yellow

Glassy luster

Fluoride replaces the substance hydroxyapatite in your teeth with more acid-resistant fluorapatite, helping prevent tooth decay.

Monazite is typically reddish-brown in color, although it can also be yellow, green, or gray.

Monazite

Mohs' scale: 5–5.5

Monazite is a unique kind of phosphate mineral that is similar to apatite. It also contains a wide array of rare earth elements that are used in technology, such as to make cell phones and electric cars. This makes monazite one of the most valuable minerals in today's world.

Tough, dense mineral with a smooth, waxy luster

Monazite crystals are often found in small, wedge- or pyramid-shaped clusters.

Chromite

Mohs' scale: 5.5

Chromite is made up of chromium, iron, and oxygen. It is the most important ore of chromium, which is an essential element for the production of speciality minerals and high performance alloys, which are substances formed from two or more metals, such as stainless steel.

Dark-brown to black color with a metallic luster

Can form octahedral, or eight-sided, crystals

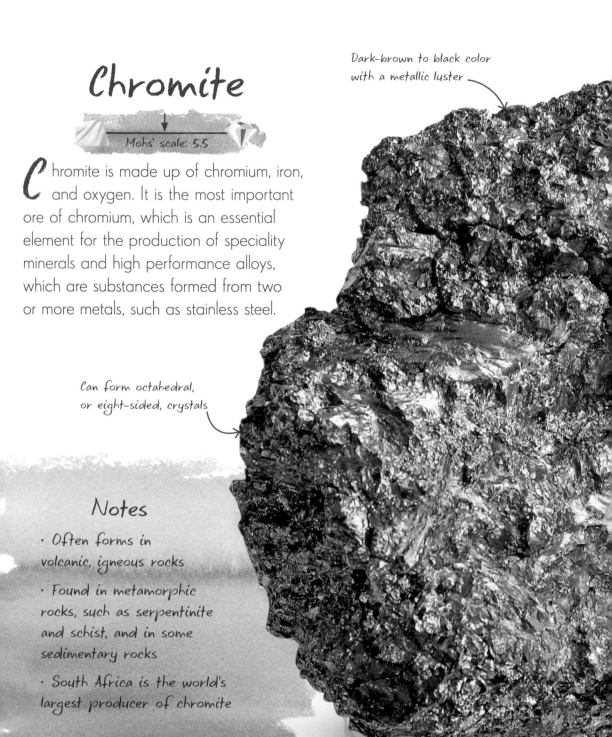

Notes

• Often forms in volcanic, igneous rocks

• Found in metamorphic rocks, such as serpentinite and schist, and in some sedimentary rocks

• South Africa is the world's largest producer of chromite

53

Sub-metallic to
dull luster

Usually black, brownish
black, or grayish green
in color

Uraninite

Mohs' scale: 5–6

A common oxide mineral, uraninite is a vital source of uranium. Uraninite is radioactive, and can be hazardous if not handled properly. If mixed with glass, however, it is less dangerously radioactive than most household electronics.

Uranium from uraninite deposits was used during the Manhattan Project, a program of research led by the USA during World War II (1939–45) to produce the first nuclear weapons.

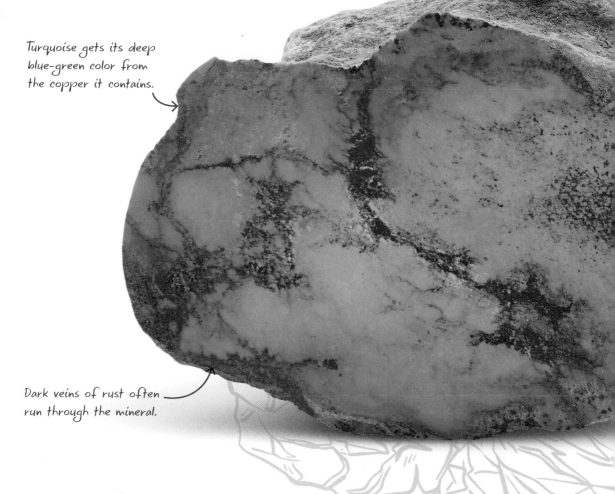

Turquoise gets its deep blue-green color from the copper it contains.

Dark veins of rust often run through the mineral.

Turquoise

Mohs' scale: 5-6

This gorgeous blue-green mineral was one of the first to be mined and cut. It is quite easy to carve, and has been used in jewelry and ornaments by many different peoples, including the ancient Egyptians, Persians, Native Americans, and the Aztecs of Mexico.

Notes

· Forms as nuggets in various shades of blues and greens depending on the amount of copper

· Today, it is mined in Iran, Egypt, China, Mexico, and the USA

Opal

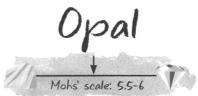

Mohs' scale: 5.5-6

Most opals are green and blue, but black opals are the most valuable. It lies buried like treasure below the surface of the harsh Australian desert. Imagine a black stone that holds all the colors of a dazzling rainbow, trapped inside trying to get out! These opals are highly revered in Australian Aboriginal culture. It's as if nature painted a masterpiece on a precious gem, just for you to discover!

Looking like a watercolor painting, opals are created through a unique combination of silica and water.

Black opals display a kaleidoscope of colors, with blues, greens, and reds swirling together.

Sodalite

Mohs' scale: 5.5–6

Sodalite is one of several minerals found in lapis lazuli, a blue stone which was once the source of a valuable deep-blue pigment. Sodalite has been used for centuries in architecture and interior design, both as ornamental stones and as tiles for flooring.

Sodalite is known for its deep-blue color, but it can also be purple, gray, green, yellow, and pink.

Sodalite is quite fragile and often contains many cracks.

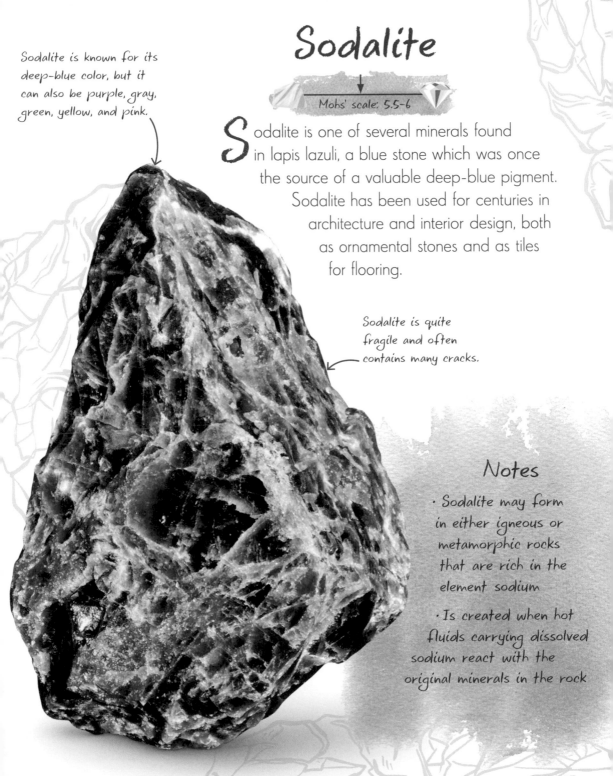

Notes

· Sodalite may form in either igneous or metamorphic rocks that are rich in the element sodium

· Is created when hot fluids carrying dissolved sodium react with the original minerals in the rock

Skutterudite

Mohs' scale: 5.5–6

The rare mineral skutterudite is made up of the metals cobalt and nickel, and also contains arsenic. Skutterudite was discovered in the 1800s in the Skuterud mines, Norway, from which it gets its name. Skutterudite is often found alongside other mineral deposits that are rich in other metals as well, such as silver, antimony, and bismuth.

Bright metallic luster and steel-gray color

Often found in massive or granular clusters

Notes

- Great potential for converting heat into electricity
- Source of cobalt, an important metal used in items such as powerful magnets and aircraft engines

Rhodonite

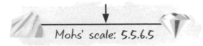

Mohs' scale: 5.5.6.5

Forming in beautiful red or pink crystals, the mineral rhodonite is mostly made up of manganese, silicon, and oxygen. It is found in metamorphic rocks, such as certain schists or skarns. The name "rhodon" means "rose" in ancient Greek, and its rose-red crystals can shine like rubies.

Usually pink or red, with a glassy to pearly luster

Forms masses of small and granular crystals

Hematite

Mohs' scale: 5-6

The tough mineral hematite is one of the most common iron ores. Its name comes from the Greek word for "blood," and the mineral is often red to reddish-brown. Hematite is found in sedimentary rocks around the world. It is also one of the main minerals on the planet Mars.

Hematite is often fine grained.

Hematite produces the natural earth pigment red ocher, used in paints and ceramics.

Notes

· Red ocher made from hematite has been found in cave paintings around 40,000 years old

· Important as the primary source of iron ore for steel and iron products

· The abundance of hematite on Mars has led it to be called the "red planet"

Small nails or paper clips will stick to magnetite.

Like a ghostly hand, the magnetic field is generated by the iron atoms inside the crystal.

Magnetite is black to brown in color, and is dense and hard.

Magnetite

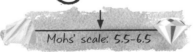

Mohs' scale: 5.5-6.5

A form of iron oxide, magnetite has an unusual characteristic. It can generate its own magnetic field! This magnetism can attract iron objects or other rocks. An important ore for iron, magnetite is widely mined in Europe, the Americas, and Australia.

Often has lines, called striations, on its crystals

Usually black to brown-black in color, with a metallic luster

Columbite

Mohs' scale: 6

The mineral group called columbite was first discovered in Connecticut, USA, and was named after the Italian explorer, Christopher Columbus, who had voyaged to the Americas. Columbite is made up of the elements niobium and oxygen, and contains varying amounts of manganese and iron.

Epidote

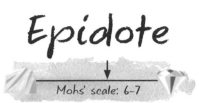

Mohs' scale: 6–7

The beautiful green mineral called epidote is found all over the world. However, it is fragile and difficult to cut, so it is more often collected as an ornamental stone than used in jewelry.

Epidote is an alteration mineral, which means it undergoes change. It starts life as a type of white mineral called plagioclase, and over time the weather changes it from white to green.

If combined with certain feldspar minerals, epidote forms a lovely pink and green rock called unakite.

Glassy to resin-like luster

Shades of green and green-brown

Minerals in myth

Throughout the ages and all over the world, civilizations have believed certain minerals had mythical powers. From the stunning black tourmaline crystals of the ancient Egyptians to the glowing labradorite of the Inuit people of Canada, here are just a few.

The ancient Egyptians believed that the long slender crystals of **black tourmaline** brought protection and healing. They were commonly used in jewelry, as amulets (charms), or in carvings.

Black tourmaline forms brittle, glassy crystals.

According to legend, the ancient Greek ruler Alexander the Great wore a belt adorned with the mineral **chrysoprase**, which allowed him to achieve stealth and invincibility in battle.

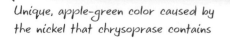

Unique, apple-green color caused by the nickel that chrysoprase contains

In Peru, the Inca people believed the mineral **rhodochrosite** was the blood of former kings and queens turned into stone.

Rhodochrosite is rich in the mineral manganese, also found in the human body.

In Mexico long ago, the Aztec people believed that **turquoise** was a sacred mineral. They associated it with the fiery sun, perhaps because of a sunny blue sky and a hot, blue flame!

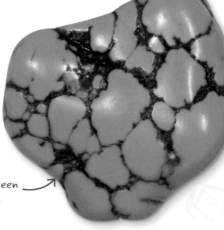

The mineral's unique blue-green shade gives its name to the color, turquoise.

In the freezing Arctic Circle, a myth of the Inuit people says that the mineral **labradorite** is made from the aurora borealis, or northern lights. The mineral is found in an area called Labrador, in northeastern Canada.

Labradorite is a variety of a mineral group called feldspar.

Labradorite

Mohs' scale: 6-6.5

Labradorite is known for the special play of light on its crystal faces. This form of iridescence is given the name labradorescence, in which a glow of color seems to appear from below the crystal's surface. Labradorite is often used in jewelry and other decorative items due to its beautiful iridescent colors.

Typically gray or black in color

The crystals have a blue-white glow, called schiller, which changes color when viewed from different angles.

Glassy or pearly luster

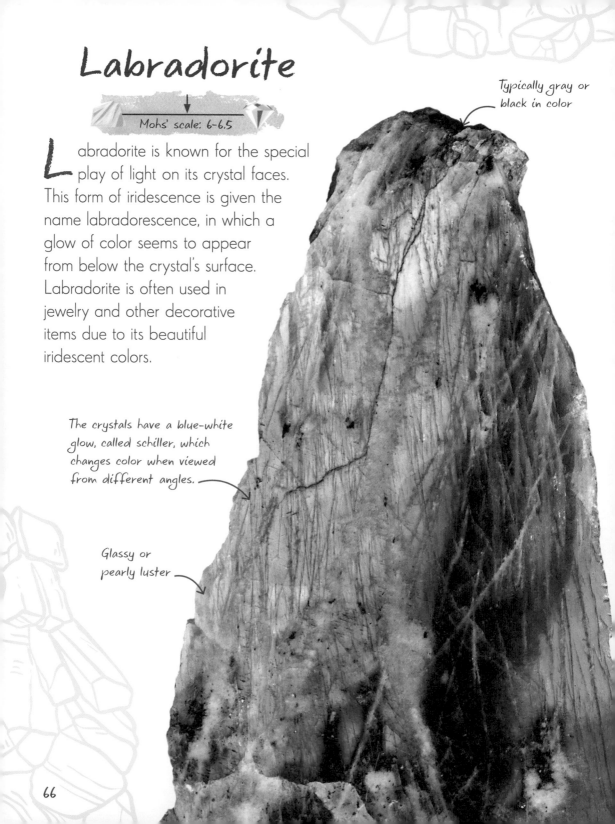

Notes

· Microcline is used in the production of ceramics and glass, and in parts for pottery kilns and furnaces

· Microcline provides the pink color in many graphites and pegmatites

· Feldspars are the most common silicate minerals on Earth

Green microcline is known as amazonite.

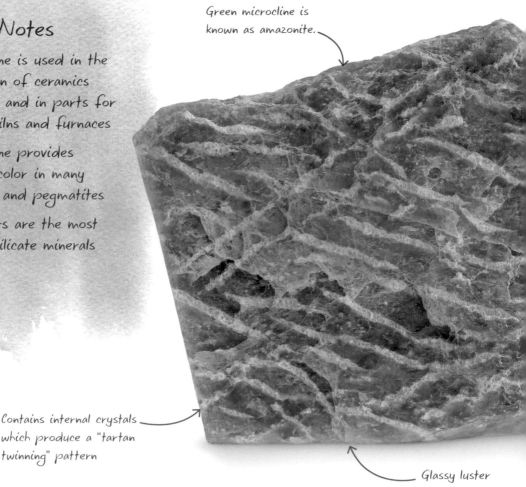

Contains internal crystals which produce a "tartan twinning" pattern

Glassy luster

Microcline

Mohs' scale: 6-6.5

Microcline is a member of the feldspar group of minerals— the building blocks for granites, the most common igneous rock in the Earth's crust by volume. Microcline feldspar displays a unique characteristic called tartan twinning, in which two or more crystals grow together in a cross-hatched pattern, a little like the cloth used by the family groups, or clans, of Scotland.

Rutile

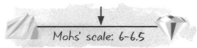

Mohs' scale: 6–6.5

This mineral is found in many igneous rocks and some high-pressure metamorphic rocks. Rutile is a type of mineral called an oxide, which means it is made up of oxygen and one or more metals—in this case, titanium. Rutile is useful as an indicator mineral—its presence can show, or indicate, that other metal-rich ores will be found nearby.

Notes

- Rich in titanium—a very valuable metal vital to the aerospace, medical, and electronics industries

- Rutile is an accessory mineral, which means it is found in many types of rocks in small quantities

- Great at bending light, rutile is used to make microscopes

Metallic luster, with thin column-shaped or needle-like crystals

Red-brown to red-black in color

Pyrite

Mohs' scale: 6–6.5

C rystals of this mineral are striking for their reflective gleam and neat faces, which look as though they have been cut with a blade.

Pyrite's name comes from "pyr," the Greek word for fire, because of the sparks it produces when struck with iron. It has been found among precious belongings left in prehistoric burial mounds.

Another name for pyrite is "fool's gold," because of its similarity to gold nuggets.

Pyrite

Gold

The crystals can be different shapes, including cuboid, which is six sided.

The finest translucent green jadeite is called "imperial jade" because of its links with the old imperial court of China.

Apple-green color, with a glassy to pearly luster

Jadeite is hard, but can be carved.

Jadeite

Mohs' scale: 6-7

This rare and beautiful mineral is highly prized for its translucent green color. It is the main mineral, the other being nephrite, that is commonly known as jade.

Since early times, jade has been carved and polished to make beautiful jewelry and ornaments by civilizations in China, Japan, Korea, and Mongolia, and by the Maya and Aztec peoples of Mesoamerica.

Sperrylite

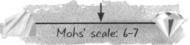
Mohs' scale: 6-7

A rare mineral, sperrylite is an important source of the metal platinum. Sperrylite has a metallic sheen and is made up of the elements platinum and arsenic.

Sperrylite was first discovered in the late 19th century in the impact crater Sudbury Basin in Ontario, Canada. Even today, Sudbury Basin is the world's most important site for the mining of this valuable mineral.

Notes

· Often found in deposits of nickel, copper, or chromite in Canada, South Africa, and Russia

· It can be challenging and expensive to mine underground, due to the depth and complexity of the deposits

· Source for platinum, used in electronics, the car industry, dentistry, and jewelry

Very hard, dense mineral with a shiny surface

Mining for minerals

Minerals occur naturally deep inside the Earth's crust. Over time, shifting continents, rising mountains, and erupting volcanoes bring a small fraction of these stony treasures to the surface. While many kinds of minerals are found worldwide, a single type of mineral is sometimes found in just one place. Here are just some of the major mineral sites across the world.

Minerals and metals

The Americas are rich in minerals and metals. This includes the Rocky Mountains, in North America, with its deposits of gold, silver, lead, and zinc. In South America, the state of Minas Gerais, in Brazil, is rich in metals, such as iron and tin, and gemstones, including tourmaline.

Silver nugget

Tricolor tourmaline

Mining for gold

China, along with Russia and Australia, is a major producer of gold. One of the country's biggest mines is Sanshandao Gold Mine, in the eastern province of Shandong.

A tunnel in Sanshandao Gold Mine

Mineral rainforests

Because of the way Earth formed over time, minerals are deposited in different amounts in certain places. Just as rainforests host different plant and animal species, so do mineral rainforests display wonderful diversity in minerals and rocks. These resources can be a huge boost to a country's economic wealth.

Cueva de los Cristales (Cave of the Crystals), Naica Mine, Chihuahua, Mexico

Opals

Most of the world's opals are mined in a town called Coober Pedy, in South Australia. The town's culture and economy are centered around the mining of opal.

The landscape of Coober Pedy resembles that of the moon.

Big Hole is a former diamond mine in Kimberley, South Africa, which was excavated entirely by hand.

Diamond mines

Diamond mining is hugely important in Africa. The central and southern African region—especially the Congo, Botswana, and South Africa—produce roughly half of the world's total diamond output per year.

Olivine

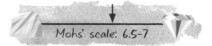

Mohs' scale: 6.5-7

Forming from magma, olivine is one of the hottest minerals on Earth. It is also one of the deepest and makes up a large part of the Earth's mantle. Olivine is a useful mineral, and is thought to help regulate the Earth's climate by reacting with water and carbon dioxide in the atmosphere. Olivine's light-green crystals can also be found in meteorites!

Notes

· Olivine is a solid mixture of two minerals— forsterite (magnesium silicate) and fayalite (iron silicate)

· Often found in iron-rich igneous rocks, such as volcanic basalt or deep gabbro

Olivine can form larger crystals used as gemstones, which are called peridot.

Olive-green colored crystals

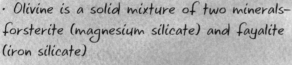

Quartz

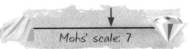

Mohs' scale: 7

Quartz is one of the most common minerals on Earth and is the backbone of many rocks. It is a silicate mineral, made of oxygen and the element silica. Its clear, glass-like appearance and beautiful crystal shapes make it popular in jewelry and technology.

Quartz is a very important mineral in modern electronics, and provides stable, reliable vibrations in devices such as watches and computers.

The color of smoky quartz comes from radiation damage to the crystal's structure.

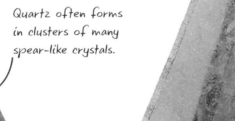

Quartz often forms in clusters of many spear-like crystals.

Hard mineral with a clear, glassy surface

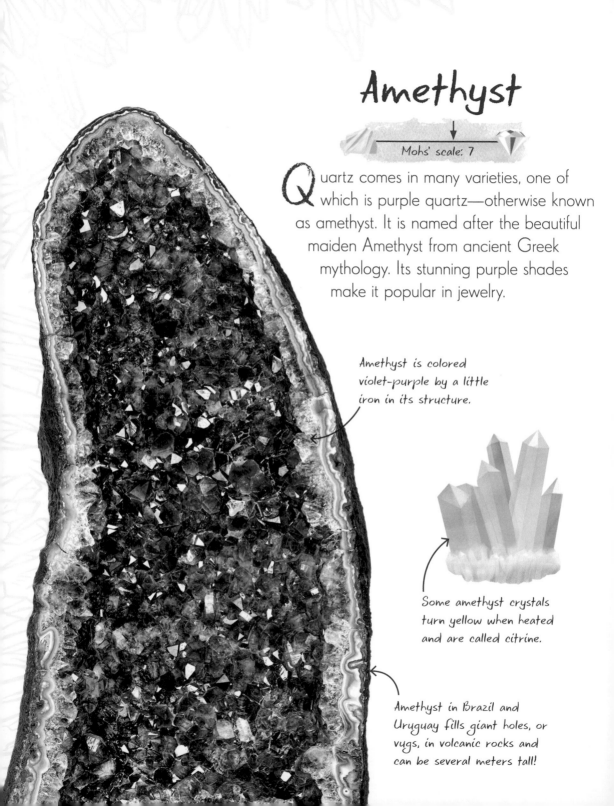

Amethyst

Mohs' scale: 7

Quartz comes in many varieties, one of which is purple quartz—otherwise known as amethyst. It is named after the beautiful maiden Amethyst from ancient Greek mythology. Its stunning purple shades make it popular in jewelry.

Amethyst is colored violet-purple by a little iron in its structure.

Some amethyst crystals turn yellow when heated and are called citrine.

Amethyst in Brazil and Uruguay fills giant holes, or vugs, in volcanic rocks and can be several meters tall!

The crystal has a
glassy luster.

Chalcedony is made up of
bands of colors, including
blues and whites.

Chalcedony

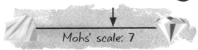

Mohs' scale: 7

Sometimes quartz crystals are so small, you would need a microscope to see them! These tiny quartz molecules, or cryptocrystalline, make up the mineral chalcedony. The mineral is formed when silica-rich water is filtered through rocks, creating tiny new crystals.

Notes

· Buried bones can form fossils made of chalcedony

· Found worldwide and is collected and polished into gemstones

· Varieties include onyx, agate, and jasper

Agate forms many dreamy shapes, from frozen clouds to lollipops of swirling color.

The bands of color are made of tiny crystallized quartz that are colored by chemical impurities.

If the bands of color are all the same thickness and are parallel to one another, this is called "onyx."

Agate

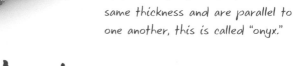

Mohs' scale: 7

The swirls of color make this stunning mineral popular with collectors and artisans, who create delicate, traditional jewelry and artifacts from it.

Agate is a type of chalcedony—a form of quartz made up of extremely small crystals and composed of many vibrantly colored layers, or bands, of silica.

Zircon

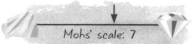

Mohs' scale: 7

The word "zircon" originates from the Persian words meaning "gold" and "color." And this commonly golden-brown mineral is one of the oldest on Earth—at more than 4.5 billion years old! Because of its age, zircon is used by geologists to help understand past events on Earth. The mineral is quite common in the Earth's crust, and is often found on sandy beaches.

Notes

· Radioactive mineral that is important in creating nuclear power

· Forms in igneous and some metamorphic rock

Zircon is a rich golden brown to browny red.

Four-sided crystal, often capped with a pyramid shape

While it comes in many shades of red, garnet can also be green, yellow, orange, brown, and black.

The shiny little red balls in this rock are garnet crystals.

Garnet

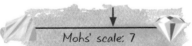

Mohs' scale: 7

Prized for their beauty, garnets are a group of hard silicate minerals with a typically red or brownish-red color. The mineral has been used to create gemstones since early times. The most common type of garnet is called almandine.

Beryl

Mohs' scale: 7.5-8

The name beryl comes from the ancient Greek *beryllos*, meaning "green stone." Its crystals are created from stacked rings of atoms that form hard column-shaped crystals.

Beryl is usually found in coarsely crystallized igneous rocks, such as granites or pegmatites. It is formed from the cooling of magma, alongside minerals such as quartz, mica, and feldspar.

Notes

· Green color comes from tiny traces of the metal chromium

· Largest beryl crystal ever found was over 59 ft (18 m) long and weighed more than 840,000 lb (380,000 kg)

· Colorless beryl is known as goshenite

Emerald is beryl in its purest dark-green form and is a very popular gemstone.

Beryl has well-formed column-shaped crystals, which can grow to several meters long.

Topaz often has a glassy luster and is found in a wide range of colors.

Forms pyramid-shaped crystals with eight faces

Topaz

Mohs' scale: 8

A favorite with many gemstone fans because of its hardness, brilliant luster, and wide variety of colors, topaz is made up of the elements aluminum and fluorine. It is mostly found in igneous rocks, such as coarse-grained pegmatites.

Topaz is formed from the cooling of silica-rich, volcanic magma, from metamorphic rocks, or as a deposit from hot hydrothermal fluids.

Notes

· Varieties range from the rare and precious imperial pink topaz to blue topaz, which is popular and affordable!

· Jewelers often treat topaz with heat or radiation to help enhance its colors or clarity

Corundum

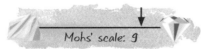

Mohs' scale: 9

O ne of the hardest minerals known on Earth, corundum is a naturally occurring oxide of aluminum.

Corundum is found in a wide variety of geological settings, including igneous rocks, metamorphic rocks, and coarse sedimentary deposits formed by rivers. As well as a gemstone, corundum is a valuable industrial mineral, with many uses ranging from heating to abrasives.

Corundum is used as a gemstone, with rubies and sapphires being the most valuable and sought-after varieties.

Red corundum is called ruby.

Blue corundum is called sapphire.

Corundum is the second-hardest mineral after diamond!

Corundum is highly durable, and resilient to the high temperatures of furnaces, kilns, and firebricks.

Moissanite

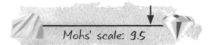

Mohs' scale: 9.5

Moissanite is the second-hardest mineral on Earth. It was first discovered in 1893 in a meteor crater in Arizona, USA, by French scientist Henri Moissan, who at first thought it was a diamond! Today, the mineral is largely grown in a laboratory, because natural moissanite is very rare and is only found in space rocks. Like a diamond, moissanite can be cut and shaped into brilliant cut gems.

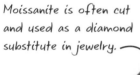

Moissanite is often cut and used as a diamond substitute in jewelry.

Moissanite sparkles like a diamond, but it is much less expensive.

Diamond

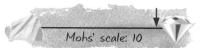

Mohs' scale: 10

Holding the top spot in the Mohs' hardness scale, diamond is the hardest mineral in nature. Diamonds form deep within the Earth at a very high pressure and temperature. Over time, they were brought to the surface by volcanic eruptions and are mostly found in volcanic rocks called kimberlites.

Notes

· Prized for their beauty, durability, and rarity, diamonds are popular in jewelry and are used as cutting tools

· Diamonds are mined in large quantities in Russia and southern and central Africa, as well as Canada and Australia

Like graphite, diamond is made of carbon, but diamond has a tightly packed crystal structure, which makes it so much harder.

Pure diamonds are made of clear, colorless crystals.

Rocks

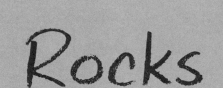

If minerals are the cells of the Earth, then rocks are the bones, muscles, and tissues that combine to make Earth what it is and what it does. Rocks are made up of almost infinite combinations of minerals, liquids, natural gases, and organic materials. They change over vast timescales, as they melt, crystallize, then get destroyed, only to later form again elsewhere. This recycling of Earth's rocks by the planet's internal processes forms a record of major events in Earth's history, and, over time, refreshes and replenishes the planet's surface with valuable natural resources.

What is a rock?

Rocks are all around us, often right below our feet! No matter where you are on Earth, swim or dig down deep enough and you'll find the hard matter that makes up our planet. Here we look at the three main types of rock and what makes each kind unique.

Igneous

Igneous rocks often form around volcanic activity. If you see a volcano erupting, you realize some rocks are born of fire — cooling from hot, molten materials called magma, created deep within the Earth. When this magma makes it to Earth's surface, it erupts and is called lava.

Columns of volcanic basalt rock make up the Giant's Causeway, in Northern Ireland.

Black igneous rock from Lanzarote, Canary Islands

Sedimentary

Imagine you see a great thunderstorm approaching. Rain falls on a mountain of sandstone, and it slowly melts away. The grains of rock move to a nearby pond, where they form a new layer. These rocks born of weathering, erosion, and deposition of sediment are sedimentary rocks.

Sandstone desert in the Valley of Fire State Park, Nevada, USA

Sandstone rock is made up of tiny grains cemented together.

Metamorphic

Over time, the burial of more and more sand and mud on top of a pile of sediment grows. As the weight piles up, the sediments change into different kinds of rock under higher heat and pressure. This is metamorphic rock.

Zebra Schist is on Kangaroo Island, South Australia.

The layering in the rock is called foliation.

89

How rocks change

The rocks that form Earth's surface layers are constantly changing into different types of rock in a process called the rock cycle. This constant cycle of renewal takes place over millions of years. It connects the three major rock types—sedimentary, igneous, and metamorphic.

Granite is a type of intrusive igneous rock, which means it forms inside the Earth.

Melting

Rocks that are buried deep underground can melt to form hot, liquid rock called magma. If magma rises close to the surface and cools, or erupts in the form of lava at a volcano, it turns into igneous rock.

Volcanic lava flow

Earth's layers

At the center of Earth is an inner core of solid metal. This is surrounded by an outer core made from liquid metal. Around this is the mantle, made from hot, solid rock. Wrapped around this is Earth's rocky crust, which is relatively cold yet less dense.

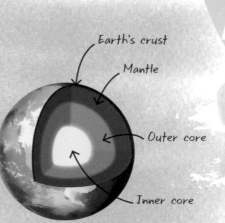

Earth's crust

Mantle

Outer core

Inner core

Marble is formed from the metamorphism of limestone.

Weathering

Rocks are gradually broken down into smaller pieces by wind, rain, and ice in a process called weathering. These tiny pieces are called sediment, and they get washed away by rivers into the sea. Gradually, they build up in layers. The pressure of new layers makes the sediment stick together.

Sandstone rock formation called The Wave, in Arizona, USA

Sandstone is a sedimentary rock composed mostly of minerals the size of sand and rock grains.

Burying

As rocks get buried or compressed deeper beneath Earth's surface, the temperature increases. This high pressure and heat changes the rocks, forming new ones, in a process called metamorphism.

Folded limestone on the island of Crete, Greece

Sedimentary rocks

Over time, rocks get worn down by weathering and they break down into tiny pieces, called sediment. This sediment gets transported to new places by wind, water, or ice, and are then deposited and buried. Eventually, this compacts and is cemented into new rock—called sedimentary rock, of which there are three main types.

Clastic

The most common type of sedimentary rock is described as clastic. It is made up of rocks created by sediment, such as shale, sandstone, and conglomerate. These have been formed from pieces of weathered rock called clasts.

The Delicate Arch in Arches National Park, Utah, USA, is made from sedimentary sandstone rock.

Chemical

Chemical sedimentary rock contains minerals that originated in mineral-rich waters. A type of limestone called travertine, for example, is made from layers of minerals in water. Chemical sedimentary rocks commonly form in caves, creating amazing features such as stalagmites and stalactites.

Stalagmites grow from the floor of caves, such as these in the Apuseni Mountains, Romania.

Fossil of an ammonite, an ancient sea creature related to modern-day squids

Biological

Biological sedimentary rock is formed from the ancient remains or activities of animal or plant life. One such rock is coal, which forms when woody plants are preserved in swamps. Other examples are hard, fossilized remains of shelly marine organisms, such as molluscs or oysters.

Sandstone

Sandstone is a form of sedimentary rock created from tiny grains of weathered rock, called clasts. These clasts vary in size between 0.002–0.08 in (0.06–2 mm) in diameter. The clasts are usually made up of a variety of hard-wearing minerals, such as quartz or feldspar. Over time, as the grains pile up in rivers and oceans, they become buried, cemented, and compacted into sandstone.

Sandstone is resistant to erosion, so it often forms ridges or hills.

The shape of the rock surfaces can show where wind or water has flowed long ago.

Layers of rock form a distinctive wave pattern in the cliffs of Coyotes Buttes, in Arizona, USA.

Siltstone

Like sandstone, siltstone is a clastic sedimentary rock. However, silt grains are tiny microscopic clasts—even smaller than sand grains. The clasts are often a mixture of clay and very fine grains of quartz. Siltstone often forms in tidal estuaries, where wide rivers flow gently into the sea. Here, the energy is low except during storms.

Siltstone may contain thin layers, or beds, of clay and quartz.

Light-colored zones contain very fine layers of quartz grains.

Dark-colored layers are made up of complex clay minerals, like chlorite or illite.

Notes

· Geologists sometimes chew silt to figure out if it is shale or siltstone—while silt is gritty on your teeth, shale is slippery

· Siltstone is less common than shale or sandstone because the environmental conditions have to be just right to create it

A dark color can be a sign that clays and organic matter, such as fossils, are embedded in the rock.

Shale often has sharp edges and splits into layers very easily.

Shale

A very common sedimentary rock, shale is made up of tiny clay-sized particles. Clays are a family of minerals that form extremely small, plate-shaped crystals. These super-small grains lie flat against one another, and this causes the rocks to slip and slide, so they break easily. Shale rocks erode quickly so often form valleys in the landscape.

Notes

• Valuable source of oil and natural gas

• Often forms in bays or oceans with gentle currents, where tiny particles of sediment get deposited and compacted

• Some shales have been found on the planet Mars!

Conglomerate

Knobby conglomerate is a type of sedimentary rock made up of large, rounded grains (clasts). Conglomerates begin life as chunky, gravel-sized sediment, such as is found in mountain rivers. As the river flows, the sharp edges of the clasts break off, creating well-rounded rocks. These rocks, separated often by finer sand, are buried, compacted, and cemented together.

Some conglomerates contain minerals such as agate, which are prized by mineral hunters.

Conglomerate is composed of large pieces of rock made up of hard, resistant minerals like quartz.

Silt and sand help glue the big pebbles together.

All about ores

When a rock or a mineral contains metals of value, it is known as an ore—and this can make the rock or mineral extremely useful and valuable. There are three main types of rock ores.

Copper malachite and azurite are found near limestone rock.

Sedimentary ores

Ores in sedimentary rocks form due to the accumulation of minerals in the rocks. This is often caused by hot hydrothermal water that has seeped into the layers of rock, such as in rock formations that contain layers, or bands, of iron.

Chalcopyrite is an important copper ore. It has a purply sheen when exposed to air.

Igneous ores

These are formed from the cooling of magma or lava, which creates new crystals made of important materials. Mixtures of valuable minerals, like copper or gold, are called porphyrys.

Muscovite can contain aluminum and potassium.

Metamorphic ores

Metamorphic ores are created by the rocks undergoing change caused by heat and pressure. For example, muscovite belongs to a group of silicate minerals called micas, and is commonly found in metamorphic rock.

How are ores used?

Ores provide raw materials for many of the products we use in our daily lives, such as in electronics, transportation, and building materials.

Copper

Copper is one of the most common and useful metals, and is used in electrical wiring.

Iron

Iron is used in building work and in materials like steel.

Gold

Gold is highly prized for its use in jewelry and electronics.

The Great Pyramid of Giza, in Egypt, is mostly made from limestone.

Often contains traces of marine life, such as fossils

Various light shades of color—especially white, gray, or tan

Limestone

Limestone is often formed from ancient fossilized shells and other animal remains found in seawater. It is a sedimentary rock made mostly from the mineral calcite. Limestone can be dissolved by acidic water, and when this happens it creates caves and sinkholes.

Dolomite

Similar to limestone, this rock gets its name from the Dolomites, an impressive mountain range in northern Italy. Mysteriously, dolomite was once common on planet Earth, but it does not form so easily today. It is found in wide shallow lakes, called lagoons, in volcanic lakes, or by sedimentary rock underground.

Dolomite forms sharp, brittle edges.

Notes

· Ore of the metal magnesium

· Unlike calcite, dolomite only lightly fizzes in acid when exposed

· The name "dolomite" can refer to the rock or the mineral

Arkose

Arkose is an unusual type of sandstone. Around 25 percent of arkose contains the mineral feldspar, while most kinds of sandstone are primarily made from quartz. Arkose forms when tiny pieces of rock sediment get buried rapidly, before the feldspar inside them breaks down. The huge rock Uluru, which rises up in the center of Australia, is made of arkose.

Mixture of sand-sized quartz and feldspar grains, mixed with other minor minerals such as mica

Usually a dirty, reddish to red-gray color

Notes

· Arkose is much rarer than typical quartz sandstones

· Highly variable in terms of its mineral content, which depends on the source of the sediment

· Arkose is the result of the unfinished breaking down and erosion of granite or gneiss, which are both rich in feldspar

Coal

Still hugely important as a source of energy, coal is a form of sedimentary rock made up of the preserved remains of woody plant material. Coal often forms in shallow swamps, rich in plant life. As trees and other woody plants die and fall into the swamps, they are preserved and buried in the mud. Heat and compaction then eventually turns the mix of clay and plant carbon into coal.

Breaks into blocky, angular pieces

When coal burns, it gives out heat and ash.

Gray-to-black color

Igneous rocks

Igneous rocks are the most common type of rock found deep inside the Earth. When volcanic lava cools at Earth's surface, it forms extrusive igneous rocks. When magma within the Earth's crust becomes solid, it creates intrusive igneous rock. Here are some of the igneous rocks that occur on, and in, the Earth.

Obsidian has very sharp edges.

Pele's hair

Pele's hair is aptly named as this kind of rock is made from thin strands of volcanic glass, which look like hair!

Pele's hair is actually made from glass.

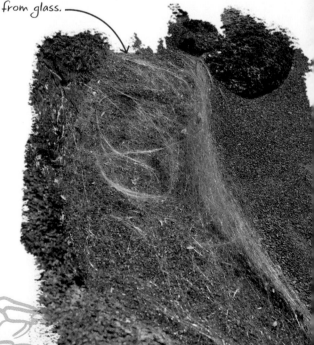

Obsidian

Obsidian is a type of glass made from volcanic activity. When volcanoes erupt explosively, magma meets air and water quickly, and freezes to create the rock.

What is a volcano?

Volcanoes originate from deep within the Earth. Hot, molten rock, called magma, rises up through gaps in the Earth's crust to the surface. If it erupts, it spews out lava, ash, and gas. As the lava flows out from the ground, mounds called volcanoes form. They come in different shapes and sizes.

Volcanic ash and hot gases escape violently during an eruption.

Magma that flows out at the Earth's surface is called lava.

Pegmatite rock containing the pale violet crystals of lepidolite

Tuff

When a volcano erupts, sometimes ash and hot gas pour down the side of a volcano. As the mixture cools, it forms a rock called tuff, which contains more than 75 percent ash.

Pegmatite

Igneous rocks containing huge crystals are known as pegmatites. They form very slowly, deep within the Earth. Here the magma forms minerals with large crystals. They are found all over the world.

Towering tuff rock formations in Anatolia, Turkey

Basalt

The volcanic rock basalt forms at or near the Earth's surface. It is made up of dark-colored iron- and magnesium-rich minerals, such as plagioclase and pyroxene. Basalt forms when hot, runny lava cools and sets quickly. The mineral makes up much of the Earth's surface and ocean floor.

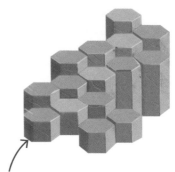

Basalt columns have formed in many places around the world that have had volcanic activity.

Vesicles (small holes) form from bubbles of gas as the lava cools.

Fine-grained crystals

Gray, brown, or black in color

Light color indicates richness in quartz and feldspar

Large crystals show that the rock cooled slowly, deep underground

Granite

Tough, coarse granite forms deep within the Earth's crust and is one of the most common igneous rocks that make up the continents. Granite is hardwearing and perfect for creating long-lasting buildings and monuments, such as Mount Rushmore, in South Dakota, USA, which has the heads of four US presidents cut into a granite cliff.

Crystals that interlock with one another suggest the rock cooled from magma.

Notes

- Granite makes up over 70 percent of the Earth's continental crust
- Over time, granite breaks down to create much of the quartz found on sandy beaches

Gabbro

Gabbro is a coarse-grained igneous rock which forms deep within the Earth's crust and mantle. One type of gabbro, called anorthosite, is even found on the moon! This rock is made almost entirely of dark iron and magnesium-rich minerals similar to basalt. Gabbro can also contain green olivine crystals.

Notes

· Sometimes used in the arts or building industry and is misleadingly referred to as "black granite"

· Highly durable, gabbro can be crushed and used to make roads

· Has very little silica, but contains a wide variety of metallic minerals that are ores of metals such as chromium and platinum

Contains large, dark minerals called pyroxene and amphibole

Has light-gray crystals, called plagioclase

Coarse crystals form
from slow cooling
deep in the Earth.

Diorite

Because of its unique mixture of white and black minerals, diorite is often called "salt-and-pepper rock." Diorite is an intrusive igneous rock—this means it is formed deep inside the Earth. It contains light-colored minerals like sodium feldspar that are rich in silica, and dark, metal-rich minerals like biotite and hornblende. Diorite cools slowly beneath the Earth's surface and, therefore, has coarse crystals easily visible to the naked eye.

Contains a mix of white and
black minerals, giving a
"salt-and-pepper" appearance

Pink, red, and tan colored

Crystals cool very quickly, so the individual grains are too small to see with the naked eye.

Rhyolite

Often causing explosive volcanic eruptions, rhyolite forms at or near the Earth's surface. This rock is chemically like granite, and contains a large amount of the mineral silica. It is made up of quartz crystals that are too small to see with the naked eye. Because rhyolite magma is silica-rich, it is sticky and traps gas. It builds up pressure until it finally explodes as hot, molten lava.

Notes

· Rhyolite magma is the opposite of basalt magma, in that it is slow, thick, sticky, and is highly pressurized

· Supervolcanoes such as Yellowstone, in Wyoming, USA, often contain rhyolite, and erupt violently as a result

Made up largely of very fine crystals, but can contain larger "floating" crystals

Can be gray, bluish or purple-gray in color

Andesite

The name "andesite" originates from the Andes Mountains in South America, where it is common. This igneous rock is also often found in cone-shaped, steep-sided stratovolcanoes, such as Mount Fuji in Japan.

Cooling quickly during volcanic eruptions at or near the Earth's surface, the magma that forms andesite is somewhere between runny and sticky—think of warm peanut butter!

Scoria

Similar in makeup to basalt, scoria is a dark, iron-rich igneous rock that forms as magma erupts from a volcano. It's quite easy to spot scoria rock since it has a lot of holes, called vesicles, on its surface. This is due to the magma cooling so quickly it causes large bubbles of gas to be trapped and left frozen in the rock. Because of all the bubbles, scoria is much less dense than normal basalt.

Notes

· Often occurs in cone-shaped volcanoes called cinder cones

· Ancient Romans used pieces of scoria, together with pumice, lime, and volcanic ash to create super-strong concrete

· Scoria is different from pumice in that it cannot float; it is also darker in color

Water seeping through holes in rock can rust the rock and turn it red.

Dark color created by iron-rich minerals

Small holes called vesicles

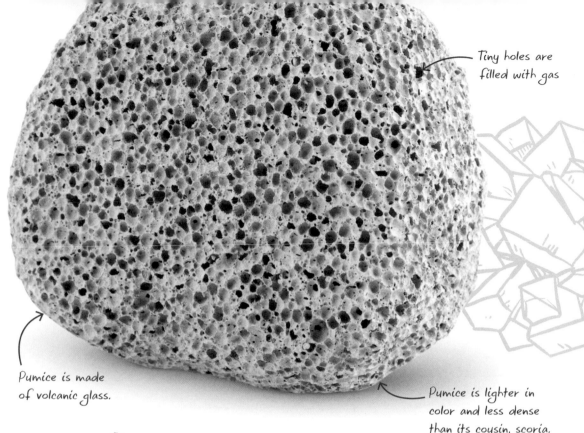

Tiny holes are filled with gas

Pumice is made of volcanic glass.

Pumice is lighter in color and less dense than its cousin, scoria.

Pumice

One of the lightest rocks on Earth, pumice forms in a similar way to scoria. During a violent, energetic volcanic eruption, a mix of magma and gas roars out into the atmosphere. The gas is trapped in tiny bubbles of glass as a sort of "froth" on top of the eruption. The pumice rock created by this mix of gas and magma is so light it can float on water. This is due to the low density of the minerals and the many holes filled with gas bubbles in the rock.

Large rafts of pumice can be found floating in the Pacific Ocean after underwater volcanic eruptions!

Metamorphic rocks

Like a soft toy might make different shapes as you squeeze it, similar forces change rocks from one form to another. When heat and pressure are applied, rocks undergo physical and chemical changes, such as turning from dark to light, or hard to soft. This kind of rock is described as metamorphic, meaning "to change form." There are two main types of metamorphic rocks: regional and contact.

Regional

Regional metamorphism occurs when large bodies of rock are buried deep down in the Earth, and undergo wide-ranging high heat and pressure. These rocks include slate, phyllite, schist, and gneiss.

Mica schist grains can be seen by the naked eye.

If slate gets buried deep down, it turns into the coarser textured, metamorphic rock **schist**. The rock's grains look sparkly because schist contains the mineral mica, which can create reflections against the light.

Glittering, gem-like quality

As the name suggests, **garnet mica schist** is a type of schist that has glittering, soccer-ball shaped garnet crystals embedded in the rock. The layers of this high-quality rock are wavy and twisted and the crystals are clearly visible.

Contact

Contact metamorphic rocks form when hot magma intrudes into colder existing rock, forming marble, quartzites, or a form of metamorphic shale called hornfels.

Hard and strong, **hornfels** is a rock that looks and feels like the horns of an animal—hence the name! It is created when fine grains of mudstone get heated up. Unlike most other types of metamorphic rock, hornfels can appear quite close to the Earth's surface.

Dark gray to brown in color

Castner Marble is a type of **marble** that formed in Texas, USA, when a magma chamber came up under limestone. Castner Marble is around 1.2 billion years old.

Layering in the marble can be clearly seen.

Slate's dark color is caused by very fine, clay mineral grains.

Slate

Dark-colored slate is a metamorphic rock formed from shale or mudstone that has undergone heat and pressure. This causes the minerals within the rock to reform, or recrystallize, giving slate the ability to be cut into thin, flat sheets. This, together with its toughness, makes slate ideal in building work, especially for roofs and flooring.

Slate was often used as a chalkboard to write on.

Splits into thin sheets

Greenish tint, and can also be gray or black

The weak, thin, wavy texture is called foliation.

Phyllite's greenish hue comes from chlorite crystals growing in place of clay.

Phyllite

Similar to slate, but exposed to higher heat and pressure, phyllite has a distinctive silky sheen and a wavy, layered texture. This texture, called foliation, occurs when minerals such as mica and chlorite grow and line up with each other within the rock. Like slate, phyllite forms through the metamorphism of shale or mudstone.

Notes

· Sometimes used as a decorative stone in landscaping and architecture

· Tiny mica crystals can make phyllite look sparkly

Gneiss

Striking because of its wavy bands, gneiss forms under very high heat and pressure as tectonic plates collide deep down underground. The bands in gneiss are caused by different minerals in the rock that have separated into distinct layers. Gneiss has a coarse-grained texture and large mineral grains that are easy to see.

Dark layers contain metal-rich minerals like biotite and amphibole.

The pinkish layer shows newly grown feldspar.

Notes

· Heat and pressure turn rocks into slate, then schist, then finally gneiss

· Sparkly rock that gets its name from an old German word meaning "spark"

· Hard-wearing and durable, so it is used as decorative stone for walls, yard paths, buildings, and monuments

Clear or light-colored layer is newly grown quartz.

Marble

Taking its name from the ancient Greek word meaning "shining stone," marble is known for its beauty. When limestone becomes very hot, over time new crystals form and create marble. Strong and smooth, marble is relatively easy to carve, making it ideal for building and sculpting.

Italian artist Michelangelo created many beautiful sculptures in white marble.

Unique veined or mottled appearance

Veining in the marble is the non-calcite minerals

Usually white, but can also be black, green, pink, and gray.

In prehistoric times, early people made stone tools out of quartzite.

Colors range from clear, to gray or tan, and can be pinkish, too!

Quartz crystals have smoothly curving crystal faces that are shaped like clamshells.

Pink or red quartzite is caused by the presence of the mineral hematite or the metal manganese.

Quartzite

Samples of quartzite can be similar to marble. However, unlike marble, which forms from limestone, quartzite develops primarily from sandstone. Quartzite is a type of metamorphic rock that is created when quartz-rich rocks like sandstone are exposed to high heat and pressure over time. The quartz crystals get fused together into interlocking crystals similar to those in igneous rocks. Quartzite has a hard, dense, and granular texture.

Bauxite

The primary ore of aluminum, bauxite is easy to spot due to its reddish-brown color and the pea-sized grains of mineral contained within it. A sedimentary rock, bauxite often forms through the wearing down of aluminum-rich rocks, such as granite or basalt, which releases aluminum into the soil. Over time, the aluminum is drained from the soil and taken by water to flat, low-lying areas, and forms bauxite.

Reddish-tan rock

Notes

- Typically found in tropical or subtropical regions, where the wearing down, or weathering, of rocks is extreme
- Source of aluminum and a soft silvery white metal called gallium
- Used in the production of abrasives and chemicals

Small and circular pea-sized grains

Rocks from space

Many rocks started their lives as molten rock within hot Earth, but not all did! Some rocks were born even earlier, and roam the solar system as asteroids, comets, space rocks, and dust. When a rock falls into Earth's gravity, it heats up in the atmosphere and becomes a meteor. And if it makes it to the ground in one piece, it is called a meteorite.

Meteorites

Meteorites are made up of rocks from a comet, asteroid, or even from another planet. The meteorite Hoba was found in Namibia in 1920—and at around 60 tons (54 tonnes) in weight, it is the largest meteorite ever found.

Hoba is too large to be moved easily, so it was just left in the place where it was found!

Gemstones from space!

Sometimes, when a meteorite hits Earth, it melts surface rock and causes it to be thrown up into the air. It then cools quickly to form a glassy material called tektite.

The gemstone moldavite is a type of tektite.

Asteroids

Rocky lumps that fly through space are called asteroids. Most asteroids travel around the sun in a broad band. This is called the asteroid belt, and it lies between Mars and Jupiter.

Vesta is one of the brightest asteroids visible from Earth.

Comets

Comets are clumps of ice and rocky dust from the far edges of the solar system. If a comet comes too near the sun, some of the ice melts and gives the comet a long tail of dust and gas.

The comet Hale-Bopp was one of the brightest comets ever seen.

Breccia rock found on the moon is composed of other, older pieces of rock.

Moon rocks

Parts of the moon's surface contain rocks that date to around 4.5 billion years ago. This is about half a billion years older than the oldest rocks found on Earth. Astronauts visiting the moon have brought rocks back with them to analyze.

Glossary

alchemist
Type of early scientist who sought how to change ordinary metals into gold

alloy
Metal made up of two or more metals

alteration
In geology, term used to describe rocks or minerals that have undergone physical or chemical changes

atom
Smallest unit of a chemical element

continental crust
Brittle outer layer of Earth that forms Earth's continents and shallow seabeds nearby

crystal
Solid substance with an orderly internal arrangement of atoms; all minerals are crystals

crystalline
Having an orderly and repetitive structure of atoms within a solid

dense
Having a large mass within a small volume; denser objects have atoms packed closer together and often weigh more for a given size

deposits
Area with a lot of minerals or rocks formed as a result of a natural process

element
Chemical substance that cannot be broken down further

erosion
Removal or wearing down of weathered pieces of rock by water, wind, or ice

evaporation
When a liquid changes to a gas

face
Flat surface on a crystal formed as the crystal grows

facet
Flat surface of a crystal, formed as a gemstone is cut

fluorescence
Ability of a mineral to give off light that can be seen when exposed to rays of invisible ultraviolet light

foliation
Repetitive layers in metamorphic rock formed as minerals line up, or split into thin sheets, due to intense pressure

fossil
Preserved remains or impressions of the bodies or actions of ancient life

gemstone
Rock or mineral that has value when cut and polished

geode
Open space in a rock, partly filled with mineral crystals

habit
Appearance a mineral takes on as it grows

halogen
Chemical element that forms a salt when reacting with metal

hydrochloric acid
Strongly acidic solution of the gas hydrogen chloride dissolved in water

hydrothermal
Description of something that formed in hot waters originating below the Earth's surface

igneous
Type of rock formed by the cooling of liquid magma or lava, either deep inside the Earth or at the surface

impact crater
Crater on a planet or larger object in space caused by the impact of a meteorite or other smaller object

inner core
Innermost part of the Earth, made up of a dense layer of iron and nickel

ion
Atom or molecule with an electric charge

iridescence
Type of light reflection that gives off a rainbow of colors

lava
Magma that has erupted at the Earth's surface

luster
Light reflected from the surface of a rock or mineral

magma
Hot, molten rock created in the mantle

mantle
Middle, thickest layer of the Earth, lying above the outer core, and made mostly of hot, dense rock

metamorphic
Type of rock formed when heat and pressure change the structure of a rock that already exists

mica
Shiny silicate mineral with a layered structure, found as tiny scales in granite and other rocks, or as crystals

mineraloid
Mineral-like material with many, but not all, of the properties of a mineral

Mohs' scale
Scale showing the relative hardness of one mineral when compared to another

molten
Object, such as rock, that is turned to liquid by heating

native
Naturally occurring metal

ore
Rock or mineral from which a valuable metal or element can be obtained

organic
Material that is created from a living thing

organism
Individual animal, plant, or single-celled life-form

outer core
Second layer of the Earth's core made up of hot, spinning liquid iron and nickel

oxide mineral
Mineral containing close-packed oxygen atoms together with metal or other ions

oxidize
To combine chemically with oxygen

periodic table
Table that shows the chemical elements arranged according to their atomic numbers

phosphorescence
Similar to fluorescence, but the mineral continues to glow after the ultraviolet light source has been removed

radiation
Energy released as tiny particles or waves

refracts
When light changes direction, or bends

resin
Type of highly viscous-to-solid organic substance found in deposits of long-buried plant life, such as amber

sediment
Weathered grains of rock that have been, or are being, transported elsewhere by natural processes

sedimentary
Type of rock formed by the weathering, erosion, and transporting of sediments that are deposited in an ocean or lake, where they are cemented and buried to form new rocks

silica
Hard material made from silicon and oxygen, which is the basis for Earth's most common minerals

silicate
Mineral containing silicon and oxygen

sinkhole
Void or dip that results from the collapse or removal of rock that used to support the surface layer

stalactite
Icicle-shaped rock formation, typically made from limestone, that hangs from the ceiling of a cave

stalagmite
Column-shaped rock formation, often made from limestone, that rises from the floor of a cave

sulfide
Mix of sulfur with one other chemical element

tectonic plate
One of many large, plate-like pieces of the Earth's crust, which move independently from one another over a very long period of time

ultraviolet (UV) light
Type of light invisible to humans that makes some minerals glow; also called UV light

vein
Narrow crack in a rock that works as a pathway for fluids, including molten rock or mineral-rich water; veins can become filled with solid minerals over time

vesicle
Small cavity, or hole, in rock, formed by the expansion of a bubble of gas or steam as the rock becomes solid

weathering
Action of wind, water, and ice that breaks down rocks into smaller pieces called sediment

Index

Senior Editor Marie Greenwood
Designer Holly Price
US Editor Mindy Fichter
US Senior Editor Shannon Beatty
Additional Design Lucy Sims, Smiljka Surla
Senior Picture Researcher Sakshi Saluja
Managing Editor Gemma Farr
Managing Art Editor Elle Ward
Senior Production Editor Nikoleta Parasaki
Production Controller Ben Radley
Art Director Mabel Chan

Editorial Consultant Selina Wood

First American Edition, 2024
Published in the United States by
DK Publishing, a division of Penguin Random House LLC,
1745 Broadway, 20th Floor, New York, NY 10019

DK books are available at special discounts when purchased
in bulk for sales promotions, premiums,
fund-raising, or educational use.
For details, contact: DK Publishing Special Markets,
1745 Broadway, 20th Floor, New York, NY 10019
SpecialSales@dk.com

Printed and bound in China
www.dk.com

This book was made with Forest
Stewardship Council™ certified
paper – one small step in DK's
commitment to a sustainable future.
Learn more at **www.dk.com/uk/
information/sustainability**

MIX
Paper | Supporting
responsible forestry
FSC™ C018179

A note from the author

A special thanks to my wife, Elizabeth Dennie, for her ideas and
assistance in making this book. To my four kids: Logan, Alyson, Morgan,
and Evelyn, who inspire me daily. To my mom and dad, who have
always supported me. And to my longtime friend and colleague
Todd Kent, my partner in crime over the last twenty-five years.

DK would like to thank:

Kathleen Teece for editorial input; Brandie Tully-Scott for design
assistance; Polly Goodman for proofreading; Helen Peters for the index;
Olivier Ribbe for the feature illustrations; Angela Rizza for the pattern
and cover illustrations.

The publisher would like to thank the following for their kind permission to reproduce their
photographs: (Key: a-above; b-below/bottom; c-center; f-far; l-left; r-right; t-top)
2 Dreamstime.com: Mehmet Gokhan Bayhan. **3 Dreamstime.com:** Wojciech Tchorzewski (b).
5 Shutterstock.com: Albert Russ. **7 Dreamstime.com:** Mirecca. **8 Alamy Stock Photo:** The
Natural History Museum (cra). **Dreamstime.com:** (ca, bc); Retouch Man . (cla); Vvoevale
(cl); Howard Sandler (cr); Bjrn Wylezich (crb); Mrreporter (crb/Calcite); Ruslan Minakryn (br).
Science Photo Library: J.C. Revy, Ism (clb). **10 Alamy Stock Photo:** Phil Degginger (cb);
Scenics & Science (crb). **Dreamstime.com:** Mara Fribus (clb); Ruslan Minakryn (cr). **11 Alamy
Stock Photo:** José Maria Barres Manuel (bl). **Dreamstime.com:** Willi Van Boven (tr); Bjrn
Wylezich (tl); Ingemar Magnusson (cl, cr). **12 Dreamstime.com:** (ca); Ruslan Minakryn (b). **13
Dreamstime.com:** (ca). **Science Photo Library:** Joel Arem (b). **14 Alamy Stock Photo:** The
Natural History Museum (br). **Dreamstime.com:** (ca, cl). **15 Dreamstime.com:** (ca). **Getty
Images:** Walter Geiersperger (tr). **16 Alamy Stock Photo:** Henri Koskinen (l). **Dreamstime.com:**
(ca, cr). **17 Alamy Stock Photo:** The Natural History Museum (cb). **18
Dreamstime.com:** (b). **19 Dreamstime.com:** (ca, c). Bjrn Wylezich (b). **20 Dreamstime.com:**
(ca). **Science Photo Library:** Dirk Wiersma (t). **21 Dreamstime.com:** (ca, b); Jiri Vaclavek
(cr). **22 Dreamstime.com:** (cb). **23 Dreamstime.com:** (cb, br). **Science Photo Library:** Dirk
Wiersma (t). **24 Dreamstime.com:** (ca). **25 Dreamstime.com:** (ca); Jiri Vaclavek (t). **26
Dreamstime.com:** (tc, cl); Bjrn Wylezich (b). **27 Dreamstime.com:** (ca); Ruslan Minakryn (b).
28 Dreamstime.com: (ca, cl); Joan Carles Juarez (b). **29 Dreamstime.com:** (ca); Mrreporter
(t). **30 Dreamstime.com:** (ca); Viktoriya89 (b). **31 Dreamstime.com:** (ca, cl); Enguerrandcales
(b). **32 Dreamstime.com:** (ca); TRStudio (b). **33 Dreamstime.com:** (ca, cr); Panmaule (b). **34
Dreamstime.com:** (cb). **Getty Images / iStock:** ala Köhserli (b). **35 Dreamstime.com:** (ca).
Getty Images / iStock: aeduard (b). **36 Dreamstime.com:** (cb); Vvoevale (t). **37 Alamy
Stock Photo:** Phil Degginger (t). **Dreamstime.com:** (cb). **38 Dreamstime.com:** (ca). **39
Dreamstime.com:** (cb); Rainer Walter Schmied (t). **40 Dreamstime.com:** (cb); Ruslan
Minakryn (t). **41 Dreamstime.com:** (cb, br); Ruslan Minakryn (t). **42 Dreamstime.com:** (ca);
Albertruss (b). **43 Alamy Stock Photo:** GC Minerals (b). **Dreamstime.com:** (ca, tr). **44
Science Photo Library:** J.C. Revy, Ism (cr); Jean-Claude Revy, Ism (crb). **45 Science Photo
Library:** Mark A. Schneider (cr, crb); Charles D. Winters (cl, clb). **46 Dreamstime.com:** (tl, b).
47 Dreamstime.com: (ca); Ruslan Minakryn (b). **48 Alamy Stock Photo:** SBS Eclectic Images
(t). **Dreamstime.com:** (cb). **49 Dreamstime.com:** (tl, tr); Bjrn Wylezich (b). **50 Dreamstime.com:**
(ca, br). **Shutterstock.com:** Albert Russ (bl). **51 Alamy Stock Photo:** Enguerrand Cales (b).
Dreamstime.com: (ca). **52 Dreamstime.com:** (ca); Rezkrr (r). **53 Dreamstime.com:** (ca, bl); Rezkrr (r). **
54 Alamy Stock Photo:** Universal Images Group North America LLC / DeAgostini (c).
Dreamstime.com: (cb). **55 Dorling Kindersley:** Holts Gems (tr). **Dreamstime.com:** (cb, br).
56 Alamy Stock Photo: Corbin17 (c). **Dreamstime.com:** (ca). **57 Dreamstime.com:** (ca, br);
Marcofinecto (t). **58 Dreamstime.com:** (ca, b). **Shutterstock.com:** aura23 (c). **59
Dreamstime.com:** (ca). **Shutterstock.com:** MarcelClemens (b). **60 Dreamstime.com:** (ca,
b); Vladvitek (c). **61 Dreamstime.com:** (cb); Roberto Junior (cr). **62 Dreamstime.com:** (cb);
Bjrn Wylezich (cl). **63 Dreamstime.com:** (ca); Enguerrandcales (tr). **64 Dreamstime.com:**
Allocricetulus (br); Bjrn Wylezich (cl). **65 Dreamstime.com:** Miroslava Holasová (bl); Ruslan
Minakryn (tl); Ismoel Tato Rodriguez (cr). **66 Alamy Stock Photo:** Phil Degginger (r).
Dreamstime.com: (tl). **67 Dreamstime.com:** (tl, cb); Losmandarinas (tr). **68 Alamy Stock

Photo: Universal Images Group North America LLC / DeAgostini / R. Appiani (b).
Dreamstime.com: (ca, c). **69 Dorling Kindersley:** Oxford University Museum of Natural
History (b). **Dreamstime.com:** (ca). **70 Dreamstime.com:** (cb); Kongsky (c). **71 Alamy Stock
Photo:** The Natural History Museum (b). **Dreamstime.com:** (ca, cl). **72 Alamy Stock Photo:**
Cynthia Lee (bl). **Dreamstime.com:** Gozzoli (cr); Bjrn Wylezich (c). **73 Dreamstime.com:** (t);
Christopher Bellette (cl); Timwege (br). **Science Photo Library:** Javier Trueba / MSF (tr). **74
Dreamstime.com:** (tc, cl); Vvoevale (b). **75 Dreamstime.com:** (tc); Howard Sandler (c). **76
Dreamstime.com:** (cra); W.scott Mcgill (l). **77 Dreamstime.com:** (clb, br); Miriam Doerr (t).
78 Dreamstime.com: (cb); Wojciech Tchorzewski (t). **79 Dreamstime.com:** (cla, cra); Ruslan
Minakryn (b). **80 Dreamstime.com:** (ca); Mrreporter (c). **81 123RF.com:** dipressionist (r).
Dreamstime.com: (cla, clb). **82 Dreamstime.com:** (clb, crb); Vvoevale (ca). **83 Alamy Stock
Photo:** The Natural History Museum (br). **Dreamstime.com:** (cla). **84 Dreamstime.com:** (ca);
Avagyanlevon (b). **85 Dreamstime.com:** (ca, cl); Retouch Man . (cr). **87 Dreamstime.com:**
Dmytro Synelnychenko. **88 Alamy Stock Photo:** José Maria Barres Manuel (crb). **Dreamstime.com:**
Rachelle Burnside (cl). **89 123RF.com:** wollertz (tr). **Alamy Stock Photo:** Frommenwiler Fredy /
Prisma by Dukas Presseagentur GmbH (b). **Dreamstime.com:** Oleksii Lukin (ca). **Science
Photo Library:** Joel Arem (tr). **90 Dreamstime.com:** (b); Proseuxomai (cr); Ekaterina
Kriminskaia (crb). **Shutterstock.com:** Yes058 Montree Nanta (cra). **91 Dreamstime.com:**
Katrina Brown (tl); Matauw (bl). **Shutterstock.com:** Aleksandr Pobedimskiy (c). **92
Dreamstime.com:** Kelly Vandellen (b). **93 Dreamstime.com:** Mark Eaton (clb); Nicku (tr). **94
Dreamstime.com:** Chris Trout. **95 Dreamstime.com:** (b); 73bats (c). **96 Dreamstime.com:**
(br); Radzh Dzhabbarov (t). **97 Dreamstime.com:** Sansam (b). **98 Alamy Stock Photo:**
PjrRocks (b). **99 Dreamstime.com:** Areg Grigoryan (cr). **99 Dreamstime.com:** (b); Vvoevale
(cra); Torriphoto (br). **Shutterstock.com:** vldkont (b). **100 Alamy Stock Photo:** José Maria
Barres Manuel (c). **101 Dreamstime.com:** (b); Zelenka68 (r). **102 Dreamstime.com:** (b);
Montree Nanta (c). **103 Dreamstime.com:** Antoni Halim (b). **104 Alamy Stock Photo:**
Michael Szönyi / imageBROKER.com GmbH & Co. KG (br). **Getty Images / iStock:**
Obradovic (c). **105 Alamy Stock Photo:** Fossil & Rock Stock Photos (cl). **Dreamstime.com:**
(t); Yurasova (br). **107 Dreamstime.com:** (b); Nastya81 (t). **108 Alamy Stock Photo:** Susan
E. Degginger (b). **Dreamstime.com:** (cra). **109 Alamy Stock Photo:** Susan E. Degginger. **110
Alamy Stock Photo:** PjrRocks (t). **Dreamstime.com:** (br). **111 Shutterstock.com:** olpo (t). **112
Dreamstime.com:** (t); Bjrn Wylezich (b). **113 Dreamstime.com:** Rob Kemp (t). **114 Alamy
Stock Photo:** PjrRocks (br). **Dreamstime.com:** Avkost (b). **115 Dreamstime.com:** (bl/
Watercolor). **Getty Images:** Marli Miller / UCG / Universal Images Group (bl). **116
Dreamstime.com:** Michal Baranski. **117 Dreamstime.com:** (b); Vvoevale (t). **118 Dreamstime.com:**
(br). **Getty Images / iStock:** mikeuk (t). **119 Dreamstime.com:** Nastya81. **120 Dreamstime.com:**
Ekaterina Kriminskaia (t). **121 Depositphotos Inc:** siimsepp (b). **Dreamstime.com:** (c). **122
Dreamstime.com:** Adischordanthryme (cr); Digitalpress (crb). **123 123RF.com:** solarseven (c).
Alamy Stock Photo: Chris Howes / Wild Places Photography (cb). **NASA:** JPL-Caltech /
UCLA / MPS / DLR / IDA (tl). **Cover images:** Front: **Dreamstime.com:** Wojciech Tchorzewski
cb; Back: **Dreamstime.com:** Gozzoli ca, Nastya81 cla, Bjrn Wylezich cra.
All other images © Dorling Kindersley Limited.